JAMESTOWN PUBLISHERS

THE CONTEMPORARY READER

VOLUME 2, NUMBER 1

a division of NTC/CONTEMPORARY PUBLISHING GROUP
Lincolnwood, Illinois USA

Acknowledgments
"Life Beneath a Blanket of Snow" adapted from "Life Beneath a Blanket of Snow" by Edward Duensing, *Country Journal,* January-February, 1994. © 1994 by Cowles Magazines Inc. Adapted with permission from the author and *Country Journal.*

ISBN: 0-89061-826-7

Published by Jamestown Publishers,
a division of NTC/Contemporary Publishing Group, Inc.,
4255 West Touhy Avenue,
Lincolnwood (Chicago), Illinois 60712-1975 U.S.A.

Printed in Hong Kong.

01 02 03 04 WKT 12 11 10 9 8 7 6 5

CONTENTS

Pronunciation Key

ă	m**a**t	o͞o	f**oo**d
ā	d**a**te	o͝o	l**oo**k
â	b**a**re	ŭ	dr**u**m
ä	f**a**ther	yo͞o	c**u**te
ĕ	w**e**t	û	f**u**r
ē	s**ee**	*th*	**th**en
ĭ	t**i**p	th	**th**in
ī	**i**ce	hw	**wh**ich
î	p**ie**rce	zh	u**s**ual
ŏ	h**o**t	ə	**a**lone
ō	n**o**		op**e**n
ô	l**a**w		penc**i**l
oi	b**oi**l		lem**o**n
ou	l**ou**d		camp**u**s

Bamboo Can Do!

Have you ever thought of building a home out of bamboo?

1 What can you do with bamboo? That's not a good question. A better question is, *What can't you do with bamboo*?

2 Bamboo is a tall, treelike grass. There are 350 different kinds of bamboo. Most grow in Asia. A few, though, are found in the United States.

3 Bamboo comes in handy for all sorts of things. It can be cut up and eaten. It can be used to make fishing poles or paper. Some people weave thin strips of it into mats or chair seats. They make curtains and chopsticks out of it. Bamboo stems can even serve as water pipes.

In a warm climate, a bamboo house makes a lot of sense.

Stronger than Steel

4 Bamboo is most amazing, though, when it is used in building. Ounce for ounce, bamboo is much stronger than wood. It is much stronger than brick or concrete or steel. If you don't believe that, think about what happened in Costa Rica.

5 In April 1991, a big earthquake struck Costa Rica. One area was hit hard. Houses and hotels collapsed like piles of matchsticks. Heaps of concrete lay everywhere. In the center of the rubble[1] stood 20 homes. They were made of bamboo. Not one of the homes was damaged. Not one even had a crack.

6 It's hard to understand just how strong bamboo is. But here's one way to do it. Picture a short, straight bamboo column. The surface area at the top is about the size of a playing card. Now picture an elephant. Let's say Jumbo weighs 11,000 pounds. What would happen if you could balance the elephant on top of the tiny column? Nothing! Bamboo is tube shaped.

---

[1] rubble: rough, broken stones or bricks

A tube is a very strong form, so the column would not bend. It would not buckle[2] or break. Isn't *that* strong?

A Real Bargain

7 Bamboo is not just strong; it's also cheap. The Costa Rican homes were built for about $4,500 each. There are reasons why bamboo costs so little. For one thing, it grows fast. A stalk of bamboo can grow up to three feet per day! So bamboo can be cut down and used after only one year of growth. A tree needs to grow for 20 years before it's ready to be cut down.

8 Bamboo is easy to cut. A hacksaw or machete[3] [mə shĕt′ ē] will do the job. And once cut down,

Lightweight bamboo is easy to pick up and carry away.

---

[2] buckle: bend and give way

[3] machete: a large heavy knife used to cut thick plants

A bamboo home can be cheap, sturdy, and attractive.

bamboo is light enough to be carried away by the work crew.

9 Bamboo is simple to use. No machines, no heavy trucks, no sawmill, no steel mill—just ready-to-use bamboo. No brick making and baking, no concrete mixing—just nice, clean, nonpolluting bamboo.

Coming into Fashion

10 A well-made bamboo home will last 30 years or more. So why don't more builders use bamboo? In fact, more builders are interested in using it. Costa Rica has a special program. It is called the National

[năsh′ə nəl] Bamboo Project. It will build 1,000 bamboo homes per year. Other countries, in Asia and Africa, are watching the Costa Rican work.

The Downside

11 So, you may ask, why isn't every building a bamboo building? Bamboo has some bad drawbacks.[4] It burns easily and fast. It is hollow, so the air inside each stalk feeds a fire.

12 The danger of fire means that bamboo should not be used for big buildings. Nor should it be used for multistory homes. The safest bamboo homes are only one story high. They have many windows and doors. If a bamboo home catches fire, the people inside must be able to get out fast.

More Headaches

13 Bugs are a big problem. Termites love bamboo. Beetles love it too. These bugs

[4] drawback: something that is not helpful and may cause problems

will eat right through a bamboo home. To prevent that happening, the bamboo must first be soaked in a special liquid.

14 Water is also bad news because wet bamboo rots quickly. Within weeks, a damp bamboo house will fall apart. A bamboo house should have a big, wide roof. That way, even if it rains the walls of the house can stay dry.

15 A final problem is how to put bamboo together. Workers can nail wood and weld steel. They can use mortar for bricks. But how do they connect pieces of bamboo? In the past, people lashed[5] bamboo poles together. Today, builders have a new method. They stick pieces of wood into the ends of bamboo poles. Then they nail or glue the pieces of wood together.

Is Bamboo for You?

16 Bamboo houses have been around for a long time. In the past, only the poor used bamboo. Richer people thought wood and bricks were better. But engineers

---

[5] lashed: tied together with rope, twine, or wire

[ĕn jə nîrz′] have studied bamboo. They have learned about its strength and other good qualities. The old ideas about bamboo are starting to change.

17 It's true that bamboo homes may never make sense in cold climates. A bamboo apartment building doesn't make sense either. But in the right place, for the right use, building with bamboo is a very smart idea.

A farmer ties bamboo into bunches.

QUESTIONS

1. What are some uses for bamboo?
2. What are the good things about using bamboo as a building material?
3. What happened to bamboo homes during a recent earthquake?
4. What are the drawbacks of building with bamboo?

2310

ARMCHAIR Shopping

Is the ease of buying through the mail worth the risks?

1 When you go to the mailbox, it's there. Sometimes it's in a plain white envelope. Or the envelope may be big and shiny. It may even come as a full-color catalog. The nice term for it is "direct mail." The other term is "junk mail."

Toss or Read?

2 Some people toss all their junk mail right into the trash. Most people, though, don't do that. They pick and choose. They throw out much of this mail after a quick glance. It holds no interest for them. But

Treasure or trash? Some people love to get direct-mail pieces. But others hate it.

other pieces look intriguing[1] [ĭn trēg′ĭng]. These are the ones that people open and read.

3 That's the whole idea of direct mail. Direct mailers want you to open their letters. They want you to read what they write and then buy something. Sometimes that seems like a pretty good idea. After all, if the item is something you want, why not buy it?

How Handy!

4 Direct-mail buying has two things going for it. First, it's convenient [kən vēn′yənt]. You can stay home and be an armchair shopper. All you have to do is write a check and lick a stamp. Or you can make a toll-free call with your credit card in hand.

5 Second, direct-mail firms give you a lot of choices. They offer a wider span of merchandise than stores do. Direct-mail firms that sell clothing or

[1] intriguing: interesting

shoes carry all sizes. Many times, local shops don't have the room to store all their goods in every odd size.

The Downside

6 There are also reasons *not* to buy through the mail. Three big problems come to mind. First, you can't inspect[2] what you are buying. That is important when you buy clothing. With good direct mail companies, this may not be a problem. They show good pictures in their catalogs and describe each item with care. Still, you can't feel the fabric with your own hands before you buy.

7 Second, costs for shipping and handling can add up. When you buy through the mail, you pay all shipping costs. These fees can sometimes be pretty steep. Some firms add on a charge for what they call insurance. That is a false fee. By law, all mail-order firms must get a product to you in perfect shape. An insurance charge is,

---

[2] inspect: look at closely

in fact, nothing more than a price hike.

8 Third, you have to wait to get what you buy. The law says that a firm must get goods to you within 30 days. But that law does not apply if the seller states a later date in print. A company can then take from five to eight weeks to get an order to you. If the seller doesn't make the deadline stated, you have a choice. You can wait for the order even longer. Or you can get your money back.

9 With good mail-order firms, these are not big problems. They deliver the product quickly, and their goods are top of the line. These firms will also return your money if you don't like the product. Some of the best direct-mail firms are ones that sell clothing, outdoor gear, and hard-to-find tools.

OUR GUARANTEE

We want you to be perfectly satisfied with your purchase. If for any reason a selection does not suit you, please return it, and we will exchange it or issue a refund without question.

To earn high marks, a direct-mail firm must sell quality goods, deliver them fast, and make sure the buyer is satisfied.

Mail-order firms that sell clothing offer a wide range of styles, sizes, and colors.

Protect Yourself

10 How can you protect yourself when you buy through the mail? Here are some tips:

11 1. Read with care what the catalog says. Photos may look nice, but they can mislead you. If an item sounds too good to be true, it is!

12 2. Find out what the company's return policy is. Who pays for shipping costs if you return an item? Many times, *you* will! But you don't need to pay for the company's mistakes. It would be the

company's mistake if, for instance, you got a shirt in a size you didn't order. The same is true if an item's color doesn't match the catalog color. Maybe the stitching on an item is poorly done. That is the company's fault. On the other hand, who is at fault if you return an item because you changed your mind?

13 3. Know the facts. If you place an order by phone, note the date and time. Write down the name of the person who takes your order. Also jot down any order number the phone clerk gives you. Keep the catalog. Mark the pages and circle the items you order.

14 4. Protect yourself when you pay for mail-order goods. The best way is to pay by credit card. That way, if something goes wrong, it is easy to cancel your debt. You might pay by check. Most of the time, that's fine. But what if you

Don't be fooled by pretty catalog photos. Make sure you know the facts about what you buy.

have a complaint about an item you get? What if the firm goes bankrupt? In both cases, the company can cash your check but not make good on your order. The worst way to pay is to send cash through the mail. Not only do you risk losing the cash—but most direct-mail firms won't take it.

Mountain of Mail

15 How many catalogs do you really want? The more items you order by mail, the more catalogs you will get. The reason is that direct-mail firms sell your name to other such firms. You may get catalogs

from firms you've never heard of. That's because your name has been sold to those companies.

16 You can put a stop to all of the junk mail. You can write to the Direct Marketing Association [ə sō sē ā′shən] in New York City. Ask them to take your name off their list. Then, *presto,*[3] no more catalogs—*if* that's what you want.

17 Most people like to get catalogs. They like the convenience of shopping by mail. Maybe you do too. But use common sense when you buy this way. You can then enjoy the pluses of armchair shopping and avoid most of the minuses.

It's easy for catalogs to pile up by the dozen.

[3] *presto:* suddenly, as if by magic

QUESTIONS

1. Name two good reasons for buying through the mail.
2. What are the risks of buying through the mail?
3. Why is paying by credit card the best way to buy through the mail?
4. How can you stop junk mail, such as unwanted catalogs?

Life Beneath a Blanket of Snow

HOW DOES SNOW ACT
AS A BLANKET FOR ANIMALS?

1 Flake by flake, snow covers the ground in winter in cold areas. This blanket can last for weeks or months. It's hard for rabbits, birds, and deer to find food in the snow. But other animals need the snow to protect them.

2 Fresh snow looks smooth and clean. Underneath, the ground is the same as it was in the fall. There are fallen trees and leaves on the forest floor. There are rock piles under the cliffs and tall grass in the fields. Short grass covers the lawns. When snow falls, it does not fill in every space. It bends the grass. It flows around trees

A hungry coyote howls on this snow-covered prairie.

and rocks. It isn't a solid block. Under it are spaces and tunnels.

A squirrel leaves its home under the ground for a breath of fresh air.

3 Under the snow, it is warmer and brighter than you might think. In summer, the sun warms the soil, which stores up this heat. In winter, the heat rises toward the cold air. If there were no snow, all the heat would escape. The ground would be frozen solid. But snow acts as a blanket. It keeps the ground much warmer than the temperature that we feel in the air.

Animals Under the Snow

4 Some animals, like the fox, may dig into the snow to make a warm shelter from a storm. But many small animals live under the snow all winter long.

5 The largest of these animals is the red squirrel. It is about one foot long and weighs less than seven ounces. Most of

This blanket of snow along the river locks in warmer temperatures below the ground.

the year, red squirrels live in trees. But when it gets cold, red squirrels build tunnels under the snow. They eat pinecones they have stored during the fall.

6 Meadow voles [vōlz], which are like mice, need snow to stay alive. Most of the year they live in burrows[1] under the surface of the ground. When it is freezing cold and there is no snow on the ground, meadow voles are in danger. The ground begins to freeze. Their burrows can't protect them from the weather.

---

[1] burrow: a hole in the ground made by animals for shelter or protection

Beneath this quiet snow scene is a small-animal world of nests and tunnels.

7 Once it snows, life becomes easier for meadow voles. The snow blanket keeps the ground warm. And the bottom layer of snow becomes loose and easy to tunnel through. Meadow voles build nests under the snow.

8 Because they are small, meadow voles must eat often to keep up their body heat. They dig tunnels near their nests and eat all the plants they find on the way. When the snow melts, you can tell where their tunnels were. There are narrow trails of very short grass.

Sharing Warmth

9 Meadow voles have many relatives. Some of these are prairie voles, pine voles, deer mice, and shrews. In warm weather, these animals keep to themselves. But in winter, they share their nests with others of their kind. Sleeping together keeps all the animals warmer. The animals take

Foxes might dig short-term shelters. But they live above the ground in the winter.

turns leaving the nest to feed. This way, the nest is always warm when they return.

10 There are drawbacks to these shared nests. It is easy for sickness to spread from one animal to another. And predators[2] [prĕd′ ə tôrz] are more likely to find the nests because of their strong smell.

The Hunters

Owls are one of many small-animal hunters.

11 There are many predators of these small animals. They include foxes, coyotes, owls, hawks, weasels, and house cats. These predators may hear or smell a vole moving under the snow. But they will have a hard time catching one.

12 The long, thin weasel [wē′ zəl] is the best hunter. It can easily dig through snow and travel along tunnels. Often a

---

[2] predator: an animal that lives by hunting, killing, and eating other animals

A red fox catches an unlucky meadow vole for dinner.

weasel will take over a nest. It will eat the animal inside and line the walls with their fur. When the snow melts, you can see these fur-lined nests. They tell the tale of life and death under the snow.

13 Shrews also hunt under the snow. They are not good diggers, so they use tunnels made by other animals. Shrews need a lot of food, so they hunt for insects. Shrews sniff to find their prey.[3] They also use their whiskers to feel prey and their ears to hear it moving.

---

[3] prey: an animal hunted and killed by another animal for food

Insects and Plants

14 Snow fleas are closely tied to winter. They are found in the northeastern part of the United States. These little blue insects live in the leaves on the forest floor. On warm days, they come to the surface of the snow. There may be enough of them to form a dark patch on the snow.

15 Snow fleas are also known as springtails because they can jump. When the temperature drops, they go back under the snow. Snow fleas are proof of life under the snow.

16 Plants get a head start on spring under the snow. Light can get through the snow and make the ground warm and moist. This lets plants live and grow. Some plants, like wild onions, push through the snow. Other plants, like snow buttercups or glacier[4] [glā′shər] lilies, even bloom above the snow.

Light can get through the snow. These buttercups will pop up even before spring.

[4] glacier: a large, slow-moving body of ice

17 As spring arrives, the snow melts. The plants and animals that live safely under the snow must get ready for the new season. There will be many challenges[5] ahead. But when winter returns, the snow will again provide a blanket to protect them. ◆

Questions

1. Which is the largest animal that lives under the snow?
2. Why do meadow voles eat often?
3. How does sharing a nest below ground help meadow voles and their relatives?
4. Which animal is the best hunter of animals that live under the snow?
5. How does light help plants under the snow?

[5] challenge: a test of one's skill, strength, or courage

THE PRIDE OF PARIS

Why is the Eiffel Tower a world-famous landmark?

1 Some people thought it would collapse on their heads. Others just said it was ugly and ruined the Paris skyline. One man hated it so much that he took a detour[1] to avoid seeing it.

2 The Eiffel [ī′fəl] Tower never did collapse. Now, more than 100 years after being built, it is a famous landmark. It says boldly to all who see it: This is Paris. Indeed, not many people go out of their way to avoid the Eiffel Tower. Instead, visitors from all parts of the world come to see it.

---

[1]detour: a roundabout way

It took two years to build the Eiffel Tower.

A Symbol of French Greatness

For years, the Eiffel Tower was the world's tallest structure.

3 In 1889, the French government hosted a huge world's fair in Paris. The fair would mark the first 100 years since the French Revolution [rĕv ə lo͞o′ shən]. During the event, the French would also show the charm and beauty of Paris. They wanted to impress[2] visitors.

4 For the fair, France built what was then the world's tallest structure. It was a 984-foot tower. In honor of its builder, Gustave Eiffel, it was called the Eiffel Tower.

5 The tower was built to show the greatness of France. It also stood for a growing faith in science in a new age. The French hoped the tower would act as a beacon.[3] Its light would invite the world to come to Paris.

---

[2] impress: to have a strong effect on

[3] beacon: a signal light

A Black Chimney

6 Work on the tower began in 1887. Nothing like it had been built before. Some builders were not happy with the plans. One professor said that the tower should not be more than 700 feet high. If it was higher, he claimed, it would fall. Eiffel felt sure that would not happen. He even offered to pay from his own pocket for any damage caused by such a fall.

7 Other people disliked the tower for different reasons. One group of artists and writers hated it. They wrote a letter of protest. It said that the tower looked like a big black chimney. The letter also said that the tower's crude looks and large size ruined views of churches and museums [myo͞o zē′əms].

8 The complaints were ignored, and work continued. The tower had three platforms, or decks. By the spring of 1888, the first deck was finished. By July, the second deck was done. And by March 1889—in time for the fair—the whole tower was finished.

9 Eiffel threw a party to show off the new tower. He asked 50 Paris leaders to go with him to the top. Because the elevators were not yet working, they had a long, long climb. Forty guests made it to the first platform. It was 360 steps above the ground. But only 20 people climbed to the top—a total of 1,652 steps.

Guests enjoyed champagne and fireworks at the top of the new tower.

10 Eiffel gave a champagne [shăm pān′] toast at the top of the tower. During a show of fireworks, he raised the French flag. Everyone could see it waving high above the city.

Facts and Features

11 The Eiffel Tower is made of wrought [rôt] iron and weighs more than 10,000 tons. Two and a half million rivets[4] hold it together. Every four years, the tower gets a new paint job. Painters use 40 tons of

---

[4] rivet: a metal bolt

paint to give it a fresh look.

12 The criss-cross pattern of iron within the framework keeps the structure steady in strong winds. Eiffel made the tower so sturdy that it never sways more than four inches. But it does grow! On hot days, the tower is six inches taller than on cold days. That's because heat causes metal to expand.

13 The Eiffel Tower held the honor as the world's tallest building until 1930. Then the title passed to a building in New York City. The new winner was the Chrysler Building.

Crazy Stunts

14 Most people want to reach the top of the Eiffel Tower for a great view of Paris. On a clear day, they can see as far as 50 miles away. Some visitors are happy to climb the stairs to get this view.

15 For a few people, though, a good view is not enough. They want an extra thrill. Over the years, the tower has inspired a lot of crazy stunts.

16 A few people have climbed the tower from the outside. Others have jumped off the top of it, using a parachute [păr′ ə shōōt]. A writer once rode his bike down one side. The tower has even been the setting for trapeze acts.

17 Surely the prize for the most foolish stunt goes to a French tailor named Reisfeldt. He thought he could fly off the top of the tower! For wings, Reisfeldt used a cape. He hit the ground hard when he fell. A doctor said that the tailor died of a heart attack on the way down.

The Eiffel Tower Today

18 As a symbol of Paris, the Eiffel Tower draws millions of tourists each year. They can see the city as elevators with large glass windows carry them to the top deck. This deck holds 800 people at one time. But on a busy day, a person may need two hours to reach the top.

19 The Eiffel Tower has its own museum, which shows films about the tower. There are two restaurants and a snack bar. The

tower also has a gift shop and space for meetings. It even houses a post office on the first level.

20 The man who designed the Eiffel tower has not been forgotten. At the base of it, there is a bust of Gustave Eiffel. His famous landmark stands for Paris itself. Eiffel's beacon will keep calling people to the beauty, charm, and genius of that great city.

Gustave Eiffel, 1832–1923

QUESTIONS

1. Who was Gustave Eiffel?
2. Why did some people hate the Eiffel Tower?
3. What makes the Eiffel Tower such a striking landmark?
4. Name two of the daredevil stunts inspired by the Eiffel Tower.

The Trail of Tears

What made the Trail of Tears such a tragic event in American history?

1 It was a sad sight. Thousands of men, women, and children trudged[1] across the land. Soldiers forced them on with gun butts. Many fell dead from hunger and cold. The Native American Cherokee people will never forget or forgive this Trail of Tears.

Quiet Lives

2 The Cherokees once lived in the Great Smoky Mountains of Tennessee. For hundreds of years, they lived quiet lives high in the mountains. The Cherokees

[1] trudged: walked in a tired way

In this detail from a painting, weary Cherokees trudge across the Trail of Tears.

hunted the woods and fished the streams.

White settlers wanted the gold found on Cherokee land in the Smokies.

3 When white people settled the land, Cherokee life changed. To try to save what land was left, the Cherokees began to live as the settlers did. Like their white neighbors, they became farmers.

4 In 1828, gold was found in the Smokies. The discovery brought heartbreak to the Cherokee Nation. White men wanted the gold. To get it, they wanted the Cherokees to move away. The settlers also wanted the Cherokee land for farming. They hoped to set up their own farms with fields these Native Americans had cleared.

5 In 1830, the United States government stepped in—to side with the settlers! The government said that the Cherokees would have to relocate.[2] They would have to move west to Oklahoma Territory and set up new farms there.

---

[2] relocate: move to a different place

6 The Cherokees did not want to move away. The Smokies had always been their home. The Cherokees asked President Andrew Jackson to help them, but he said no.

Troops Arrive

7 In 1838, United States troops came to the Smokies. They began to round up the Cherokees. Only 1,000 Cherokee people got away. They hid deep in the mountains. The rest of the Cherokees were caught.

8 Soldiers dragged men from their fields. They pulled women and children from their homes. The troops showed no kindness to the frightened Cherokees. The soldiers shouted at them in English. It was a language many Cherokees did not understand.

This is a drawing of a Cherokee man in the early 1800s.

***The Trail of Tears* (1942), an oil painting on canvas by Robert Lindreux [lĭn′ drō]; Woolaroc Museum, Bartlesville, Oklahoma**

9 Soldiers forced the Cherokees into stockades[3] and split up their families. Some children wound up in camps far from their parents. The soldiers did not care. They had orders to move the Cherokee people.

A Long, Hard March

10 When the camps were filled, the long march began. Armed soldiers put the Cherokees into 17 large groups and pushed them west. About 15,000 Cherokees set out.

---

[3] stockade: a pen made with tall stakes to hold prisoners or animals

11 The march was grim[4] from the start. The Cherokees were herded onward like cattle. Some were shoved into wagons. A few rode on horses. Most of the people had to walk. They did not have enough blankets or warm clothes. Many did not even have shoes.

12 Children cried as they waved goodbye to their mountain homes. Men and women also cried. As one Cherokee said, ". . . all look[ed] sad like when friends die."

13 Oklahoma was a thousand miles away.

---

[4] grim: cruel or harsh

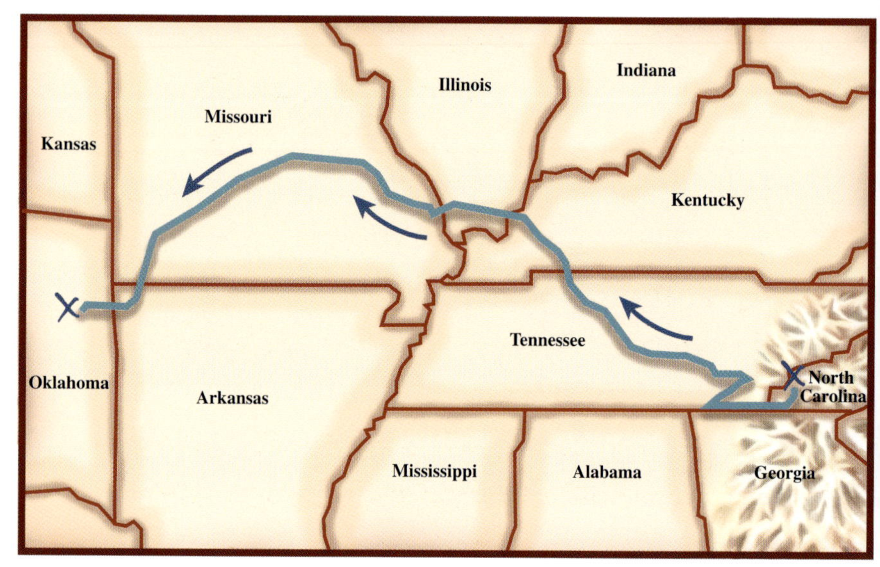

Soldiers forced the Cherokees west along the Trail of Tears to Oklahoma.

To get there, the Cherokees had to tramp through mud and dust. They slogged[5] through rain, sleet, and snow. John Burnett was a soldier on the march. He later wrote about that time. "The sufferings of the Cherokee[s] were awful," he said. "The trail of the exiles[6] was a trail of death. They had to sleep in the wagons and on the grounds without fire. And I have known as many as 22 of them to die in one night. . . ."

---

[5] slogged: plodded on at a steady pace

[6] exile: a person forced to leave home or country

Death on the Trail

14 Some people died from the cold. They shivered and shook but could not get warm. At last, their bodies ran out of heat. Others, too tired to keep going, died from exhaustion[7] [ĭg zôs′ chən]. Still others died from disease; they were too weak to fight off sickness.

15 Hunger was always a problem. The marchers had only the food they could carry with them. Their grain sacks got wet and were soon filled with bugs. No one had enough to eat. They all grew weak. Many Cherokees starved to death.

Cruel Treatment

16 The soldiers saw the pain and death they were causing. Yet they kept the groups of Cherokees moving anyway. It was hard for old people to keep up the pace. The heartless soldiers whipped them to make them move faster.

17 Mothers with young children struggled along.

---

[7] exhaustion: completely tired out

Burnett told of one woman with three small children. She set out ". . . with a baby strapped on her back and leading a child with each hand." As Burnett told it, "the task was too great for that frail mother. . . . She sank and died with her baby on her back and her other two children clinging to her hands."

18 There was no time to give the dead funerals or burial. The soldiers forced the groups to keep moving. Bodies of the dead were thrown into ditches dug along the trail.

19 After about six months, the march ended. The Cherokees had reached Oklahoma. By then, 4,000 people had died. More than one fourth of those who set out died on the Trail of Tears.

In Oklahoma, Cherokees had to start new lives in a land unlike their old home.

A Different Life

20 The Cherokees looked at their new land. It was not at all like their old home. The land was flat, dry, and hot. The Cherokees had to start new lives. But they never forgot the horrors of the long march. They named it the "Trail Where We Cried." Today it is called the Trail of Tears. The trail still marks a sad chapter in United States history. ◆

QUESTIONS

1. What was discovered in the Smoky Mountains in 1828?
2. Where did the government say the Cherokees could live?
3. What problems did the Cherokee people face during the march?
4. What happened to the marchers who died on the way to Oklahoma?

Water from the Heavens

Why was the world's most fabulous waterfall a well-kept secret?

1 Have you ever been to Niagara [nī ăg′ rə] Falls? It is a dazzling sight. No other falls has such a great amount of water. The water flow of Niagara Falls is twice as much as that of the next largest falls.

2 But Niagara is not the world's highest waterfall. Its greatest drop is 167 feet. In height, Angel Falls in Venezuela [vĕn ə zwā′ lə] wins. It is 3,212 feet high. That makes Angel Falls nearly 20 times higher than Niagara Falls!

With its steep 3,212-foot drop, Angel Falls is the highest waterfall in the world.

A Lost World

3 Angel Falls is not easy to find. No outsider knew of it until 1935. That year, a mapmaker from Venezuela saw the waterfall from a plane. Until then, only the Pemón [pĕ mōn′] Indians had seen it. They lived in this little-known region of South America. They knew how to find the falls on foot. They kept their secret for centuries[1] [sĕn′chə rēz].

4 The secret was not hard to keep. The Pemón live in a remote[2] part of Venezuela. The land is thick with rain forest jungles. The rivers run white and wild from steep, flat-topped mountains.

A Pemón woman washes clothes by the river.

---

[1] century: one hundred years
[2] remote: distant

Colorful birds, like this toucan, also live in rain forests.

Naming the Falls

5 Angel Falls is named after Jimmy Angel, an American bush pilot.[3] In 1935, he was nearly broke. One day, Angel's luck changed. A stranger asked Angel to fly him into southeastern Venezuela. He would pay Angel $5,000. That was a lot of money in those days. The pilot jumped at the chance.

---

[3] bush pilot: one who flies a small plane into rough country, landing on any open flat area

Angel Falls is on the Churún [cho͞o ro͞on′] River in Venezuela.

6 It was a bumpy flight, but the two men landed safely. Angel soon learned why the stranger wanted to make the trip. The man knew where to find a river filled with gold nuggets.

7 In just three days, Angel and his passenger had sifted and strained 75 pounds of gold. This was all the extra

weight the plane could carry. So the two men packed up. Angel was thrilled. He would have enough money to last a long time. Besides, he was sure he could always come back for more gold.

Discovery

8 Jimmy Angel never saw the stranger again. Two years later, in 1937, Angel was ready to fetch more gold. This time he flew alone. But without the stranger, he could not find the river of gold. He looked and looked but could not find it. This wild land seemed to stretch out forever. From the sky, it all looked pretty much the same.

9 When Angel saw an area that looked promising, he crash-landed his plane. He did not find the river of gold. Then it took him 11 days to hike to a village. But on his way, he stumbled across the highest waterfall in the world. Jimmy Angel was the first outsider to see it from the ground. Today it bears his name—Angel Falls.

Sky High

10 The Churún River flows across the flat top of Auyan-Tepui [ŏ o͞o′yŏn tĕ′pwē]. Auyan-Tepui is called Devil's Mountain in English. Suddenly, the river jumps out over a steep cliff. The water falls 3,212 feet, barely touching the rock wall. That drop is higher than two Sears Towers on top of each other!

11 During the dry season, the Churún River is low. So not much water goes over the falls. Then, the water is no more than mist[4] by the time it reaches the bottom.

Visiting Today

12 The land near Angel Falls is still wild today. On foot, it is still hard to get close to the falls. But four hikers got *very* close in 1971. They climbed up the sheer rock face behind the falls. It took them 10 days.

13 Most people don't go that far. Still, they like to get as close as they can. Guides lead visitors to the base of the falls. It takes two or three days of hiking to get to the base on foot. It is very tough going.

---

[4] mist: a fine spray of water similar to that of light rain

The Churún River's 3,212-foot leap from Devil's Mountain was named Angel Falls.

The path is steep. The air is hot and sticky. Hikers walk the path in darkness. The sun does not shine through the thick roof of trees and plants of the jungle.

14 Visitors can't be sure they will see much when they reach the base of the falls. The region is often covered in clouds and fog. Many people wait for the clouds to lift. For some, the wait pays off.

Visitors can get the best view of Angel Falls by airplane.

15 The best way to see Angel Falls is still by plane. A flight to the area leaves every day. The planes can get very close to the falls. They often fly just 100 yards from the cliff. If it's sunny, the sight of these mighty falls is one no visitor will ever forget.

Questions

1. In what way does Niagara Falls beat Angel Falls?
2. Why did Jimmy Angel agree to fly the stranger into the mountains?
3. Why didn't Angel and the stranger take home more gold?
4. What happened when Angel tried to find the river of gold a second time?
5. Why is it still hard to visit Angel Falls on foot?

You can act out a feeling. The feelings you can show range from sadness to joy, from love to hate. You need not make a sound, but your audience[1] [ô′ dē əns] will get the message.

2 A mime gives just such a silent performance. The story told without words is also called a mime. Mime is a very old way to entertain an audience.

---

[1] audience: those watching or hearing a performance

A mime invites viewers to "listen" to his silent story.

An Ancient Art

3 In long-ago times, large crowds went to open-air performances. Today, thousands of people still go to open-air shows. But long ago, there were no microphones and sound systems. Only a few people could hear the actors onstage. So the art of mime was born.

4 Mimes exaggerate[2] [ĭg zăj′ ə rāt] body language. Their actions can be understood from a distance. Sometimes the mime wears a mask. A painted mask with a very fierce [fîrs] frown can be seen better than an angry face. Again, a big crowd can easily follow what is going on. Masks also help the mime performers in another way. With different masks, one performer can take two or three roles in a mime play.

5 In long-ago times, just as today, audiences loved a good story. Before radio, films, and TV, there was mime. From ancient Greece and Rome to India and Japan, stories were told in mime. All

---

[2] exaggerate: to make something much bigger or greater than it really is

over the world, mime is an old way of telling stories. Many people today still love to watch a mime performance.

6 Mime is not just for big theaters and huge audiences. Traveling street mimes kept the art alive in Europe during the Middle Ages.[3] Back then, the Christian

This street mime leaves his silent world to take a break.

church felt that dance, plays, and mime were wrong. Today, we have all kinds of entertainment. Sometimes a church even puts on its own shows. There are still many street mimes today.

---

[3] Middle Ages: a period in Europe's history from about A.D. 500 to A.D. 1450

Basic Styles

Charlie Chaplin based his art on the Italian style of mime.

7 Not all mime is the same. Each culture has its special style. There is, for example, the Oriental style. This style is very detailed. The mime performer wears wigs and makeup. Props and music are also used. The mime must be a good athlete. Some of the moves are like those of a gymnast[4] [jĭm′nəst].

8 The Japanese Nō[5] theater has performed for 600 years. It mixes mime with dance, poetry, and song. All the actors are men.

9 The Italian style of mime is quite different from those of Asia. There is no special makeup or props. Each mime can add his or her own special style. Have you ever seen a silent movie? The comic stars used slapstick humor. These stars

---

[4] gymnast: an expert gym athlete

[5] Nō or Noh: Japanese drama. From the Japanese word *no*, meaning "talent"

were from the Italian school of mime. Two of the most famous silent movie comics were Charlie Chaplin and Buster Keaton.

10 The French have yet another idea of mime. The French mime puts everything into black and white. The face is painted chalk white. The clothes hug the body. Black and white are the only colors for clothes. The movements are lifelike. But they are not simple. A French mime might show a walk down a street in 20 ways. Michael Jackson's "moon walk" was a form of mime walking. He seemed to be going forward. But he was really moving backward!

What It Takes

11 Being a mime is hard work. It's a lot more than just making funny moves and faces. The best mimes study their art for years. A mime must also stay fit. He or she follows a set pattern of exercises. These are done to tune up face and body control.

12 A mime must be creative. To create a character [kăr′ək tər], a mime must think like an actor. What is the character feeling? How can that feeling be shown? Slowly, piece by piece, a character evolves[6] [ĭ vŏlvz′].

Marcel Marceau

Marcel Marceau creates a world without words that everyone understands.

13 One famous mime character is a clown named Bip. He was created by the great French mime, Marcel Marceau. Marceau uses Bip in many skits. Bip's face is white. His sweater is striped. He wears a single flower in his hat. Bip does many funny things. He walks against the wind. He struggles to hold on to balloons. He tries to escape from an invisible[7] box.

14 One of Marceau's skits is called "Youth, Maturity, and Old Age." It shows the effect

[6] evolve: come about little by little
[7] invisible: not able to be seen

of age on a person. Marceau does it with one silent flow of moves. At first, he moves with youthful grace. Then he grows up. He shows this with slower body moves. At last, Marceau slows way down as he becomes an old man.

15 Marcel Marceau can create a whole world onstage. He doesn't need props. And he doesn't need words. He was once asked why his act was such a hit. "In a world that is so loud," Marceau said, "silence is a balm[8] for the soul." ◆

QUESTIONS

1. Why was mime popular in the ancient world?
2. Why did mime almost die out in Christian Europe?
3. What are the differences between the basic styles of mime?
4. Why is it difficult to become a good mime?
5. Who is Marcel Marceau?

[8] balm: something that soothes or heals; a comfort

Pirates of the Past

Why were people afraid of the Vikings?

1 They came by sea. Their ships moved swiftly up and down Europe's coast. When these sailor-soldiers landed, people screamed and ran for cover. The warriors[1] were the mighty Vikings. From A.D. 800 to A.D. 1100, they terrified Europe. They raided and burned towns and churches. They killed men, women, and children. During the age of the Vikings, no one along the coast of Europe felt safe.

[1] warrior: a fighter

Vikings became the most feared raiders of their time. What they could not steal, they burned.

Life in the North

2 The Vikings came from the north of Europe. Their homes were in Scandinavia[2] [skăn də nā′vē ə]. The people there were called Norsemen, or Northmen. The weather in Scandinavia is cold and icy. Yet the people made good lives for themselves. They knew how to live through the long winters. They put up sturdy wooden homes and wore warm clothes of wool or animal skins.

3 Norsemen raised cattle and sheep. They kept bees for honey, which they used to make their own wine. For fun, the Norsemen wrestled and played chess.

Vikings at Sea

4 Some Norsemen turned to the sea. These warlike sailors were called Vikings. They wanted adventure [ăd vĕn′chər] and riches. They left their homes and set out in ships.

---

[2] Scandinavia: Denmark, Norway, Sweden, and often Iceland and Finland

Most Norsemen were farmers. They built homes and villages near rivers that flowed to the sea.

5 The Vikings were very good shipbuilders. Their ships were as long as 95 feet, yet they were fast and lightweight. Huge sails helped the Vikings use the wind. If there was no wind, they rowed. Each ship carried 40 to 60 men.

6 The Vikings sailed far to the south. They could cover thousands of miles. Along the way, these pirates looked for places to stop. They rowed their ships into bays and staged quick raids on the nearby towns.

7 The name Viking comes from that behavior. The word *vik* means "bay" or harbor. To "go a-viking" meant to go in search of bay towns to attack.

Attack!

8 Viking raids were bloody. Vikings struck without warning. Their ships made no sound as they slid into a bay. Vikings liked to attack at night while people slept. They used swords and axes to kill anyone in their way.

9 Sometimes they spared young men and women because they wanted them as slaves. After a raid, the Vikings sailed home with their captives.[3]

10 Vikings also brought home all the loot[4] they could carry. They took gold from churches and stole horses and pigs from fields. They made off with jewelry, cattle, and food.

Viking raids for cattle and riches were cruel and quick. Victims had no time to defend themselves.

---

[3] captive: someone held prisoner

[4] loot: something stolen or taken by force

Far from Home

11 The Vikings attacked towns in England. They hit Belgium and raided Italy and Spain. In A.D. 886, they surrounded Paris, France. The King of France gave them a huge treasure to spare the city.

12 More and more people were living in Scandinavia. This growth left little new land to farm. So some Vikings sailed away from Europe. They looked for new places in which to live and trade goods. They set out in their open ships to cross the Atlantic Ocean. The Vikings were sailing into unknown waters, but they did not mind. They were fearless; they just set their sails and headed west. A Viking explorer named Eric the Red set out this way in 982. He sailed west from Iceland and made it all the way to Greenland. A few years later, his son

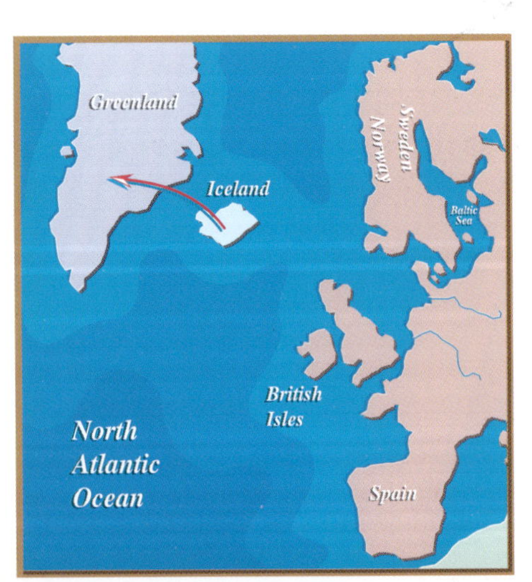

Eric the Red sailed west from Iceland to Greenland.

Leif Ericson, called Leif the Lucky, landed on the east coast of North America.

went even farther west. The son's name was Leif [Līf] Ericson. Ericson sailed to Newfoundland, Canada. He was the first person from Europe to see North America.

No Fear

13 The Vikings were terribly bold; they were raised to be that way. Boys trained to be brave. Parents did not care if their sons couldn't read or write. But they wanted their boys to be strong. Young boys were taught to ski, row, and ride horses. They spent hours running and jumping. They learned to use weapons as soon as they could hold them.

Wednesday was named in honor of the god Odin.

14 Religion also helped Vikings to be brave. Vikings believed in many gods. The chief god was Odin, who lived in a special heaven. It was called Valhalla [văl hăl′ ə], or warrior's heaven. The only way that humans could enter Valhalla was to die in battle. So the Vikings did not see a battle as something scary. Instead, it was joyful—a chance to go to Valhalla.

Taking Chances

15 Because they did not fear death, Vikings took many risks. They steered their ships by the sun and stars. Even when fog hid the stars, the Vikings kept moving. They let their ships drift until the skies cleared. That is one reason they discovered so many new lands.

16 The Vikings were smart as well as brave. They didn't trust only in luck. On

long ocean trips, they brought ravens with them. These birds are known for their skill at finding land. When Vikings didn't know where land lay, they set a raven loose. Then they sailed in the same direction as the bird flew. That explains why a raven is pictured on the Viking flag.

17 In time, the Viking Age passed. But the memory of these fierce warriors has not died. Life today still carries links to these pirates of the past. For example, you might think of Vikings the next time you hear of someone going *berserk*. That word comes from the Viking Age. A crazed Viking warrior was called a *berserker*. ◆

QUESTIONS

1. What was life like for people in Scandinavia?
2. What did it mean to "go a-viking"?
3. What did Leif Ericson do?
4. What made Vikings so fearless?
5. Why did Vikings take ravens with them on long sea journeys?

YOUR WAY TO HEALTH

Why do we feel happy after a good laugh?

1 How many times a day do you laugh? Ten times a day? Five times? Or are you such a sad sack that you never laugh? If that's true, you need to lighten up. Scientists [sī′ən tĭsts] now say that laughing is good for your health.

All Work and No Play?

2 An adult laughs about 15 times a day. But most children laugh 50 times a day. Why? Because children spend much of their time having fun and doing silly things. They play—and they laugh.

When it comes to laughing and playing, children are experts.

3 Adults, though, are loaded down with real-life duties. They work all day. They pay bills and keep the car running. They have to do laundry and get the kids to school on time. In short, adults are busy. When do they have time to laugh?

4 Doctors say that adults should *make* time for fun. These experts have studied how feelings can change a person's health. They know that having fun is important. But getting patients to enjoy life is not easy, say the doctors. Adults don't place much value on play. Too often, having fun is seen as a waste of time.

One Person's Way

5 In 1979, Norman Cousins wrote a book called *The Anatomy*[1] *of an Illness*. It was about Cousins's fight with a deadly disease. He didn't want to stay in bed and feel sorry for himself. Instead, he tried to look on the bright side. He made humor a part of his daily treatment.

---

[1] anatomy: the parts of the body or thing and the way they are put together

Adults often forget to make time to play.

6 Cousins's idea seemed to work. His health improved, and he felt better. He lived 12 years after he had first become ill. Other sick people followed his lead. They, too, tried to laugh through their pain. They hoped that a happy frame of mind *would* help heal an ailing[2] body.

Old Idea, New Proof

7 The claim that laughter can heal is not new. Some doctors held that belief as early as the 1300s. They saw a link

[2] ailing: sick

between the health of the mind and that of the body. One such doctor was Henri de Mondeville [ôn rē′ də mônd′vĭl]. He thought that joy in his patients' lives would improve their health. He told the family and friends of his patients to "cheer them" and "tell them jokes."

8 Why is the healing power of laughter once again news today? We now have proof that laughter is good for the body! Until a few years ago, that idea was just a hunch.[3] Thanks to Norman Cousins, doctors now have some hard facts about laughter. Cousins spent his last years studying laughter as medicine. He worked with doctors at the UCLA Medical Center to research humor. Together, Cousins and the doctors learned more about *how* laughter heals.

Even doctors long ago felt that a cheerful heart helped heal the body.

[3] hunch: a strong feeling about what will happen

9 Doctors found that laughing gives more strength to the body's immune [ĭ myo͞on′] system. This system helps the body fight disease. The immune system contains "killer" cells. These cells try to kill harmful cells that enter the body. Laughter makes the job of the killer cells easier. When a person laughs, the body reacts. This reaction sends special chemicals [kĕm′ĭ kəlz] all through the body. That action, in turn, readies the immune system to fight off germs.

Laughter As Exercise

10 Think about how you feel after a good workout. You may be a bit sore and tired, but you feel wonderful. Long distance runners say that they even feel "high" after a few miles. Laughter has the same effect; it feels good to laugh.

11 Indeed, laughter is a kind of exercise. Think about your last big laugh. How did your body react? You threw back your head and took a deep breath. Blood rushed to your brain. Maybe you felt a

little giddy.[4] You were not worried about your tax bill or your next trip to the dentist. You could feel the stresses of daily life drain away.

12 What's more, your pulse rate and blood pressure[5] [prĕsh′ər] went up as you laughed. Then they came down again and were lower than before you laughed. Cousins called laughter "internal jogging."

13 One study shows that 100 laughs do the body as much good as 10 minutes of rowing a boat. In other words, laughing gives the heart and lungs a good workout. In that sense, laughter is a bit like jogging—but without the sweat. This is the kind of workout you can enjoy while lying on the couch watching a funny TV show.

Group Giggles

14 Annette Goodheart wrote a book on the power of laughter. She, too, says that humor can improve a person's health.

---

[4] giddy: dizzy or silly

[5] pulse rate and blood pressure: measures of blood flow within the body

Once you get the giggles in a group, it's hard to stop them.

She thinks that laughter may have the strongest effect on people in a group. When people laugh, they are in touch with themselves. Shared laughter makes people connect with each other. That's why laughter so often spreads to others in a group; it breaks through the feeling of being alone and apart from others.

Limits of Laughter

15 Goodheart warns that laughter is not a cure. It won't stop AIDS or the common cold. Yet it may help a person to heal, or feel better. Laughter offsets[6] the stress

[6] offset: to make up for something else

Experts now say that good health *is* a laughing matter!

caused by illness and worry. A sick person with reduced stress feels better in both body and spirit. Laughter can help a person heal. It can make even a dying person feel better.

16 No amount of laughter or medicine can keep a person from dying. But laughter is vital[7] while we are alive. Fun and laughter do not just happen by themselves. You can look for reasons to have a good laugh each day. Unhappy people say that they can't laugh when

---

[7] vital: of life or death importance

they don't feel happy. "You have to make laughter a priority[8] [prī ôr′ ĭ tē] in life," Goodheart says. "You don't play when you feel better. You feel better when you play." ◈

QUESTIONS

1. Why do many adults find it hard to laugh and enjoy life?
2. Who was Norman Cousins?
3. What did Henri de Mondeville tell the families and friends of his patients?
4. How does laughter change the body?
5. Why does laughter have such power over people in a group?
6. What are the limits of laughter?

---

[8] priority: something that is given attention before something else

PHOTO CREDITS